All You Do Is Perceive

Also by Joy Katz

Poetry

Fabulae
The Garden Room

All You Do Is Perceive

JOY KATZ

Four Way Books
Tribeca

Please direct all inquiries to:
Editorial Office
Four Way Books
POB 535, Village Station
New York, NY 10014
www.fourwaybooks.com

Library of Congress Cataloging-in-Publication Data

Katz, Joy, date
[Poems. Selections]
All you do is perceive / Joy Katz.
pages ; cm.
ISBN 978-1-935536-35-2 (alk. paper)
I. Title.
PS3611.A79A78 2013
811'.6--dc23

2013004424

This book is manufactured in the United States of America and printed on acid-free paper.

Four Way Books is a not-for-profit literary press. We are grateful for the assistance
we receive from individual donors, public arts agencies, and private foundations.

NATIONAL
ENDOWMENT
FOR THE ARTS

This publication is made possible with public funds from the National Endowment for the Arts

State of the Arts

NYSCA

and from the New York State Council on the Arts, a state agency.

[clmp]

We are a proud member
of the Council of Literary Magazines and Presses.

Distributed by University Press of New England
One Court Street, Lebanon, NH 03766

For Rob and Chance

CONTENTS

Notes

Esse est percipi (aut percipere)
To be is to be perceived (or to perceive)

— Bishop George Berkeley

WHICH FROM THAT TIME INFUS'D SWEETNESS INTO MY HEART

When the lead crystal hangs dully,
    In the wondering as I write this,
        During the carboniferous period,
            Having finished the *meze*,

After the dog goes back to bed,
    In the continual hum,
        After we buckle on our parachutes,
            As ash settled over Brooklyn,

When the Moors ruled in Europe,
    Next summer maybe,
        After the morning hosts uncross their legs,
            Every four to six hours,

That becomes a basket tossed weightlessly
    On the day we adopted a boy,
        When I step off the quickly dropping elevator,
            After the seclusion of the cellarage,

The night before I left for college,
    During intermission,
        When someone with a clipboard called our name,
            At the ideal time,

Pending fire department approval,
    When I turn to the sink for a minute, the light switch,
        Often, hungry for marvel,
            After nothing in process can come transforming,

And then, one day,
           What seemed fair in all the world,
                      Before the tap water discolored,
                                During the oiled sound of a dog dream,

In the sun's year on earth,
           Oil, boil, squeak, uplift
                      In the evenings,
                                In the far back of the drawer,

During the cocktail hour,
           Eventually will I
                      After I have come down the hill and up the hill
                      Eventually,

After we have had a few lessons,
           At night my mother,
                      When she first entered the air,
                                In the equalsign of an allowed hour,

When the power went out,
           Every so often,
                      After the woken up and gone returned
                                When I asked her how she saw herself,

After my son has kissed me the more times,
           That becomes a basket tossed weightlessly
                      As the opposition receives non-lethal assistance,
                      In the wondering as I write this,

On a pleasant spring day,
  This hour, for example,
    Now, passing between my shoulderblades,
      Before the jury deliberates,

After four minutes (at sea level),
  As I grow bigger in the wanting,
    As I ride around on blue ikat,
      At the urgent intervention of ground troops,

When my father returns from Africa,
  On the anniversary of
    When he gets his genius back,
      After three sets of reps,

As you began treading these long thresholds,
  As Ho Chi Minh witnessed our signatures,
    After the woken up and gone returned
      Before the music stops,

When I try remembering her voice,
  In 1978,
    "What next?" you say,
      In the middle of a budget battle

That becomes a basket tossed weightlessly
  As a baby is handed through the air to us,
    In the final seconds of the fourth quarter,
      Halfway through the preface,

After they set us on fire,
    It was time for a
        Tomorrow,
            When the sugar is dissolved,

Before the poet begins his third ode,
    Till at last, pop!
        When I understood there was a chance,
           —Which intifada was that?

Again.   Again.   Again
    (in the patience of),
        Before you can say it's cool as measuring salt,
            Whenever we rushed to the embassy,

When it was noon,
    In the middle of the night,
        In that hour of my life, to have
           A moment, so plastic,

As I stood at the foot of her bed,
    A basket tossed weightlessly
        Long after the data is useful,
           While thou on press'd flowers dost sleep,

As he meets with the rebel leadership,
    Midway through the onrush,
        As the lead crystal spins dully,
           Until she solved the difficulty,

Some thirteen years ago in a gale of wind,
    On a foil packet of shampoo,
        After a prayer with no words,
            When a spoon leaves a firm imprint,

During the last known hours,
    As the meltdown hit groundwater,
        When we signed off on everything,
            And then, a face: the woundable face of a boy.

DEATH IS SOMETHING ENTIRELY ELSE

Department of Trance
Department of Dream of Levitation
Department of White Fathom
Department of Winding
Sometimes my son orders me lie down
I like when he orders me *lie down*   *close your eyes*
Department of Paper Laid Gently
Department of Sound of Sheets of Paper
                                        he covers me with
then sings
I like best the smallest sounds he makes then
Department of This Won't Sting
Am I slipping away
Department of Violet Static
as if he were a distant station
Department of Satellite
My child says *you sleep*
Department of Infinitely Flexible Web
and covers my face with blankness
Department of Tap-Tapping the Vein
Department of Eyelash
I can't speak
            or even blink
                              or the page laid over my face will fall
Department of Clear Tape in Whorls and Double Helixes on the Wall
He says *Mama don't look*
Department of You Won't Feel a Thing
I cannot behold
Department of Pinprick
He will not behold
Department of Veils and Chimes

of Lungs Afloat in Ether

I like this best
Department of Spider Vein
when I am most like dead
and being with him then, Department of Notes
Struck from Thin Glasses Successively at Random
I must explain to my child that sleep
                        is not the same as dead
Department of Borderlessness
so that he may not be afraid of
Department of Fingertips Lightly on Eyelids
so I can lie and listen
not holding not carrying not working
Department of Becalmed   faint sound of him

                                      I am gone

His song is the door back to the room

I am composed of the notes

MY LIFE

None of the tools was in decent condition.
I had no letters of introduction
nor any passion for grand untested opportunity
and the tailors insisted
one dress couldn't work in desert, glacier, and deep-sea milieus.
That was a most influential miscalculation in history.
I traveled all over the place in little carts:
no one commanded such a mutinous crew.
For a long time, despite agriculture, despite the peasantry,
I resisted alien desires.
Naturally I found it difficult to make a career at court.
I retained my dogmatic purity, but was accessible to Frenchmen
although I had no formal training in horse latitudes.
Eventually I put forth a treasury of facts and tediously gathered specimens.
For this I was condemned as godless.
Ominous lightning-flashes, bitter dragons, famine—
I brushed off their sycophancy.
I was guided by hints and cautions
and a storm from the citadel of truth.
A deft mastery of bells kept me going.
I was the first to accept payment for my poems
(other people in other places had tried this)
and was welcomed into the salons of certain experts.
Eventually I found every place no one had yet been:
not one was the country I had come in search of.
I looked around for a spot to plant the flag I had designed, spun
        the silk for, and woven.
Four men seining for fish in the shallows
looked up at me a moment and went back to their nets.

WE ARE WALKING INTO THE SUNSET

Look, I say, pointing to the odd gold haze as if we were audience to a rare show getting rave reviews. You keep talking.

The sky is getting louder, how can you not hear it—?

Look, I say, as if I held a shovelful of earth in which all things turn and all things shift. Amazement like a taste of metal. You

keep talking. Look, I say, as if by not looking you are assigned an eternity of only talk, as if by not looking you were dooming all of us, but especially me, to scumping along like a spider on a—

Look, the sky has become stained glass made of meat!

You keep talking, as if in utter faith that life will go on forever.

Yet that in itself is lovely. Keep talking. What is more of a pleasure to see, a moon as big as a bison head or the face of a friend, talking?

SUICIDE CASCADE

The saddest time in my life was also the time the most people said,
    You look beautiful.
There was a poet I would meet for coffee, he was married,
he wanted to know would I have an affair, would I, what was I doing
he eyed my well-turned runner's legs

                        There was a poet who killed herself

The last time I saw her she made a wide generous gesture, arms outswept,
in a room where people stood strapping tape on cartons full of books.

"Four dollars," said the poet, swung
her arms as if she were walking through a field
of empty Saturday nothing-to-do—

The saddest time in my life was also the time I wrote about furniture,
    the heavier the better.
A butcher block says *live here.*
Says fish on ice, knife marks, steady steady, loaves of bread.

I mailed myself back from a crater.
                  Weighted myself
to the heavy legs of tables
waited for a place to change the ending.

The poet tried to reach her therapist before she killed herself
is a place you can change the ending.

Open her book to the poem about the
evidence, you want ambulance, you want knife marks you want serious,
    you want serious you want hard rain, noise, turbines, thumbnails.

Come to a party! someone says to a woman who resembles me
exactly, feature for feature, but isn't me
                                        on the saddest day of my life
I sit cross-legged at a party, pretend to eat a piece of pie.
Pie, what world is that from?

                            Turn back one page
to a safety
pin or a spring
                Saturday that would keep you
from walking up to the edge of that poem.

Four dollars, said the poet
four dollars in a meadowful of cows
                        four dollars we are aiming toward heaven
four dollars shakespearing over earth's curve

16

A WOMAN OF WORTH

Proverbs 31

A woman of worth who can find
For her province is far above rubric

A woman of wood, hooks, and rind
The forks have gone suddenly ruthless

The ~~hearth of the~~
~~husk of the~~ husband

She dogs him, she evolves
Dislodges god the last days of her life

A woman of words: who could mind
So what if her rupees surprise us

She is fond of her housefly
Her housefly is cloned with garnet

She consoles a friend yet bests him
The fruit of her hands is vincible

A woman of wound who can find
She gilds her lawn in streaks, makes song her law

Her hands hoist the splendor, the spilt
She strews her hands toward the pool

"A woman at war with her mind"
(It is vividly 1966)

She counts singers in fields, and bison
Steak and doubloons in her cloud chamber

She opens her mouth: a kingdom
Its likeness on her tongue

A woman reorders, combines
Chills rise up into her breast, blessing the husk, singing

Favor is false and beauty is vain
Flavor is pulse and bedding is vale

This woman yet fears the lord, praise her
Praise the wood, praise the intimate grain

WHEN I LOOK AT ARCHITECTURAL MODELS

I fix upon their many whites: of talc,
of institutional kitchen, the silver heads of ladies
as baby pear trees on the promenade.
In the atrium, light of a saltwater aquarium
filled with sardines swimming
hard into a barrel-shaped current.
These foam-core walls are the temperature of skin.
This mall will house 99-cent stores and check-cashers   someday
but today is cradled
in the arms of the architecture student
on her way to crit. She nudges a soffit (size of a teaspoon)
upward by a sixteenth-inch; that twitch
equals a shipment of ductwork in a custom diameter;
the contractor will miss his wife's daughter's
quinceañera making calls all day trying to source it;
and then, in Guangzhao, a fabricator . . .
I could crush this city block over my knee.
                                        How perfectly
each wall enacts the one outside my window:
a building, a simple arrangement of lines
vanishing into perspective.
And then sun comes and strikes the brick, turning it into
        soiled lace. . . .

STUDY OF A FRIEND WITH ONE BREAST

1

She is not a cello,
not a pear.

2

The nipple is a houselike form
composed of nearly straight lines.
It is dark brown.

3

A crack in the wall behind her
of a winglike precision.
It moves from her left hip
to her right shoulder.

4

The scar is not ruched.
It is not unbreast.
It arcs slightly, pointing to her right ear.

5

She is beautiful because she has a breast. No.
Because of her wet hair—no,

6

(Sound of soap dropped
on hollow porcelain)

7

Her skin: nacre, wet snow:
No,

8

Her body is perfectly dry.
Her shadow is a long shape on the floor.

DECEMBER, FEVER

A tang approaches, like the smell of snow.
Illness like a color deepens—
pale gray, thick-in-a-cloak gray, secret coat silk,
and finally the weight of rough pelts heaped on the bed.

The last enchantment of the day is tearing pages out of a book.
The paper soft and thin, like falling asleep
(a hand backstage smoothing my hair:
the school friend, Lakamp, became an undertaker)

My baby laughs to rip the pages.
Stays by me, does this damage.
The tearing moves like voltage through my own hands.

> *Oh mother skimming fever*

I need him to linger

> *are you still happening there, in your body?*

I just want to lie at the edge of breaking.

Yes, I am still backstage, here in my body.
The baby pulls out another page—
leaving him would come this easily.

I will bind myself to the thinnest sounds,
the feather coming out of the pillow.

Please keep ripping up the words.
Please don't need anything from me.

TO A SMALL POSTINDUSTRIAL CITY

—where day empties into a wide boulevard: not so deserted it becomes interesting, not ruined into beauty. Not celebrated. No genius sermons. Some boarded-up buildings, a store with plain bread in plastic. I grew up here. Nothing charged, nothing trying to look old or too pretty. Some flowers. I get a great, blank feeling, driving. I'm a girl, driving. Poems aren't labor, progress, robber barons—not poems. Four men sit in recliners on a grand side lot. Lush weeds, what grows without regard. Girls' names no one thinks to pick: Lorraine. Here is the street where I lived. Where I can be—nothing. Four p.m., light rain, no one asks what I am writing. A room lovingly painted sends its notions into me.

HE LAUGHS TOO HARD ABOUT THE WINE

He laughs too hard about the wine.
The fish glisten rawly on ice.
He laughs loudly, not noticing her slight recoil,
a feeling she accepts in herself as proper (but the idea nicks her, "proper").
Their friends concentrate on the long menu.
If she could see through the table, she would see their limbs side by side,
a pair of keels, unperturbed, still holding within themselves
the possibility of motion, precise and electric.
                                        From where there is no suffering,
from where there is just the clean feel of blade cutting into flesh
comes the server:
"Needlefish and amberjack."
In their friends' faces, the trace of something—sorrow?
They have passed under a bridge that left its shadow on their teeth.
(The fish: thick, pale, solid and wet as a wall of weather)
He laughs too hard, a waiter drops a platter.
He can't feel it,
how she must hold to everyone and swim them to the same shore.
He laughs as if there were no shore.
She pulls away—opposite of photographs in albums: lovers, friends,
all clasping, their heads are suns, their arms the rays of suns.
His laugh says: nothing got us, not the dark, not loneliness.
His laugh sounds to them (she thinks) like plates breaking.
(Blue bowls hold the shape of cupped hands)
Beyond the edges of the room, nothing;
beyond the room: space, weather, the rain, nothing.
Then a voice full of indifference that feels like true north:
"Needlefish and amberjack."
                        The server holds her pen
as the couples look up from their menus, faces like sails struck by sun.

THE LETTUCE BAG

The luckiest lettuce comes in a plastic sleeve that expands, weblike, to cradle the largest red leaf or the smallest butterhead. If a rose were the size of a head of romaine, its petals would be held unbruised. The lettuce bag would not distort the most bouffant beehive hairdo; indeed, you could slip it over an actual beehive—a small one—and its grid of plastic tethers would barely impress the delicate wax. If labias were in season, their tender interiors, their roundness, would be touched by the grocer's mist. The lettuce bag has the same selflessness that a good translator has for a French poem. The little plastic sleeve moves me like a suffragette! But I am being too grand. Abundantly soft and pliant, its perforations clean, the bag has a modest beauty. In the modern refrigerator, though, lettuce goes limp as a peignoir unless stored in an astronaut helmet.

THE FAMILY, ONE WEEK OLD

The parents, as if clubbed between the eyes
but with no memory of it, regard the infant
who has no self-regard and none for them.
It gazed into the world and shat:
it will not have such independence again
                                    until old age.
Where did the baby come from?
La la, Mother sings.
Father has it on his forearm, king;
baby swims, no fear of falling.
Self-forgetfulness means one has a self to forget,
grown big and bruised as a pear. What joy
when it disappears!

A ROUND PORCELAIN JAM POT, PAINTED ORANGE

A round porcelain jam pot, painted orange, with two leaves on its stem (stem = tip of a porcelain spoon).

Oranges—the real ones, fruit—are dyed that color; a ripe orange actually is greenish.

This napkin printed with a realistic bamboo pattern.

Bamboo shoots look nothing like the parent plant, but more like acoustical tiles,

which look like themselves. No one likes them. But people with drop ceilings are happy that upstairs arguments are muffled into dove calls.

When she cries, the wife is beautiful. Everyone in our building says so.

Beneath our acoustical ceiling, a ceiling of pressed tin, painted over many times, embossed with fleurs-de-lys that have lost the crispness of the irises they resemble.

Iris! Clear-eyed spear point!

The Victorians covered flowerpots with wax-dipped cotton string arranged in branching patterns, to simulate coral.

The upstairs couple hang a wreath on their door, huge rustic crown, hairy with moss, of a scale suitable for a harvest supper in D.H. Lawrence.

The barns fallen down in Ohio are the most beautiful on earth. They look like the wreckage of ancient roller coasters.

These fields were once the floors of lakes. Now, in snow, they look like the ocean floor.

You can buy trilobites in a store that also sells polished stones, moths mounted and framed, and recordings of surf that will lull you to sleep.

Not because they sound like surf, but because they sound peaceful.

The old Ohio barns have been razed, the barn siding sold to people who pay a premium for reclaimed wood. They build new houses out of it, or cupboards and shelves,

as if the proudest claim on a tree were to hold first editions and pottery (a jam pot shaped like an orange).

Some books aren't books. *Swann's Way*, hollowed out, holds two hundred dollars in small bills. *Alice in Wonderland*, letters from my father and an article about rescue dogs.

Rescue dogs—as if they weren't just plain dogs from the pound but dogs that leapt from burning buildings. Or as if they saved you when you leapt: eight dogs pulling a net taut with their mouths.

BIG BABY

Scraping sounds, metal straining, and a baby—gainly, smooth-skinned—enters the world with its canyonlike spaces and big things going wrong. And quick big things too: shadows from hopping toads on streets dry as pancakes. Even the raspberries hang heavy-lobed; the twigs make sturdy sounds of lovers pulling up to long tables. Three balloons on waxy cord float upward. Welcome! Take big steps. (The baby brings its feet down with aplomb.) No one whispers; voices ring from loudspeakers on utility poles. Welcome also to the large-and-quiet world: simple shape of mountain, fat emeralds, carven alphabet block, rhinos gliding smoothly on dolleys. In the light and air, clouds move bigly over the baby's arms. I speak to it in complete sentences. The baby gains a natural understanding of civics, geologic time, and Canada. It helps itself to large portions and slips about with whales, having learned to swim in wide shallows. I try for endearments that are not diminutive: my bus, my tarmac. What a relief to crush *tiny* underfoot into an expanse of sand on which you can find pounds and pounds of whelk. To raise up a house of timbers and catch in it bucketfuls of clear soup. To cart the empties to the dump and listen with equal pleasure to Wagner and Crispsparkle. To prefer autumn's bigger name, fall, and its battering change.

PACKING TAPE

Descendant of Puritans, packing tape vouchsafes little intelligence of its overseas journeys. In the desk drawer it's mum,

set to do the job. As my father asks no questions of his breakfast: "It fills the stomach."

Prepare to bind mightily the flaps of your box. (Inside, some fragile thing afloat in shredded paper.)

With the first pull the roll makes a hurt growl. Strap the long sides fast and the tape sounds like fish slapping a deck. Ease the last inches round the edge, hear child-hands patting wet sand. The roll's spaniel teeth bite off any length with mean precision.

Now, even if you drop it down the front steps, the box will harbor its contents.

A hundred cartons, sealed thusly, gleam in moving vans—the sole glamour of packing tape being its shine, slick as lip gloss on a teenage daughter.

HABIT

The box . . . maybe the baby will play with the box, and she can sit, not carry, not pick him up.

He does. Dreamily. Opens the plastic lid . . . He examines the lip of the box, where it clicks shut. He slowly, slowly pulls a piece of paper through a thin slot on top.

At first being alone with the baby and the box is a dim, half-conscious satisfaction, like running your fingertips over the dry skin of your feet. He turns the box over in his arms. She gives him a necklace, it falls through his hands like milk. He licks the metal clasp, and her scalp, filigreed all over, electrifies. She comes a little awake.

When she holds out the box he will bubble and tree and ha and silence, he makes sounds that run over her back like mice, sounds that cause the thinnest pins to vibrate—that are the silken, grooved edge of a guitar string not even being touched.

Now she must daily use the baby to feel this feeling: a needle afloat on plain water.

In the world of the box and the necklace there are no words, there is no appetite, there is not sex: his sounds take sex away. Is she blameless? Is the box a form of love? If you walked in and saw her, it would be that scene in the movie where the boyfriend opens the door and day has passed into night and he finds her on the floor: dull spoon, burnt match, used up.

THE IMAGINATION, DRUNK WITH PROHIBITIONS

Childhood is more embarrassing than *child*.
Girlhood is more embarrassing than boyhood.
Black is less funereal in patent,
wine more linguistic than water—
a wineglass is more secular than a minaret.
Both are welcomings for the onset of blessings,
        both are longings.

Which is more embarrassing, *daughter* or *mother*.
Religion is more embarrassing than faith.
Blessing is more embarrassing than religion
(you have to stand very still, a mother's hand on your head).
Watching someone have faith, close up,
is harder than watching them chop off a finger.

Horseback is more masculine than bareback.
Bareback implies a young girl, or a daughter.
Daughter is less enchanting than *sun*.
Morning is less interesting than waking:
morning is more birds, more pouring, more oval;
waking could be to an era, could be a crashing.

Womanhood is more embarrassing than *manhood*.
If the woman is old, breakfast is hopeless.
If breakfast is brioche, it becomes less frightening.
Insouciant is more French than nuance,
disappointment more French than matinee,
London more suave than Paris.

Welcome, *ancien régime*!
Electrified cities, cities of courtyard and iron!

Cities are always redeeming. But
private is steamier than *public*
if by private I mean a pine grove while the crowds
are busy admiring the tulips.
And if by public I mean beheadings
it is better than anyone reading about my girlhood.

Shame implies a covering of feathers, purposeful hiding
in shadow for a reason hard as iron.
Hurts wants an upgrade to *pain*—
pain sings a continuum, a line we all hang our shirts on.
Hurts demands a benediction
(my head unbearably still beneath your hand).

If the woman is old, she has a courtyard full of lions.
In this way I make her less shameful.
If she is naked, I will clothe her with *sculptural*.
Sculptural marries *body*.
Marriage is less hobbyist than *husband*,
husband more dignified than buttons.

Naked is more enticing than prayer
unless you mean an old lady.
I meant to say a courtyard full of iron, all hard lines,
against which grandmother becomes pure texture.
Texture is less embarrassing than skin
the mottle of a tidal pool—tepid calcite backwash—

I meant to say courtyard full of sirens
and spinning lights. Enough with the old woman.

In my mother's 1935 American College Dictionary, between "holocaine" and "holocene," I come upon "holocaust." It sounds cross and bored, a child about to tantrum. "Pestilence. Locusts," I read. The holocaust sits there humming like a bee-box. "From the Greek *holokauston*," I read, "burnt offering." Mad glare. "Wholesale destruction." Little holocaust kicks the kitchen chair.

I decide to take the holocaust around the town where I live. See, that's light, I explain. There are plants growing. Whole yards, people, a calm world. From inside my jacket that swarming sound. I walk the holocaust carefully back to the car. I take it to see an action movie, thinking crashes and bombs will seem like family. It goes into the bathroom and sets the towels on fire. Should I bring the holocaust home to show my mother? I do. She stops chopping onions for a minute. Don't let that thing get too close to the curtains, she says. On the street the holocaust tramples the flowers, eyes some old trees hungrily. It is a terrible nuisance. I hold it and let it beat its arms against me.

THE VERY LAST MOVIE ABOUT THE NAZIS

When they leave the camp,
just drop it, like a boy drops a stick,

they leave the gramophone.
Tapped their cigarettes   tap   tap tap

right there, blotter idle on the desk. Nazi pens
lived rightly all this time

as the stems of plants.
Ruin-men: come in and touch the pens.

Make curlicues, trace coffee rings.
The pencils smell like water. Break them

like the necks of violins.
Your wrists are thin, ruin-men

as the bridges of violins.
(Cue a high sound, run it under empty bunks,

run it under savior tanks—a saving sound.
Now cut the soundtrack. Music *out*.)

Look here, a stack of enemy 78s.
Side one shines like a headful of clean hair.

The ruin-men touch their fingers to the grooves.
My cell phone chirps   chirps   trills—

"Before we died, we heard such lovely music playing,"
sing the ruin-men, in my ear.

In the next frame, coat hems full of rescued spoons.
Poems stirred from scraps of prison yard. *Fin.*

On the F train home, the ruin-men
are in my bag. They climb the strap.

Fluorescent light flatters their craggy skin.
Ruin-men, I'll wash your feet, take you to school:

hallways thick with backpacks
and gleaming heads, comics, electronics, magnificent

ice planets, buckets of white glue.
All right? You'll be my show-and-tell.

The ruin-men get off instead at Tenement Street
to walk the plank of filmic Jewish gloom.

A naked sink backs itself against the wall.
Turn on the water, then! You won't get shot.

In the officers' club at Terezin
(we are far, far past the last scene)

you can have drinks, watch the History Channel.
Ruin-men: I would join you, but I have a migraine.

A Polish boy is waiting to take your order.
The barkeep, bored, is brushing out her hair.

[NOON, F TRAIN]

Noon, F-train. Mid-chapter. Book propped at good angle, jacket on lap. No need to rush as the conductor calls your stop. In your cove by the doors, the air neither too warm nor too cool, there is time enough (for it is a long train, the length of two city blocks, and it is coming to a slow, slow halt) to find your bookmark, tuck it in to the page. To close the book, to reach between your knees for bags, taking care not to bump, with your head, the woman doing sudoku. Remain seated: face soft: from the ambergris inside the whale, from the killing fields, move. Move from the room punctured with crystal, into the moment (it is coming) (it is still far off) when you will rise, and exit. There is time enough to adjust a scarf, even to untwist a shoulder strap. Time enough to take down a thatched roof, close a piano, pack the ammo, fold the sails, load the home, "one's earthly sac," where you have lived simply, onto a dolley, so that you can (not quite yet) pass up into the world and leave nothing behind. . . .

THE COMPOSER

In the café, a composer sits with a manuscript of sheet music. I can tell he is serious. I know he will be quiet. I take the table next to his.

Then I am hungry for the notes, clear as crows in winter; the staves are a track I passed over in winter. No words, high over fields, looking out a cold dot of window.

My mother married my father, and not the others, because he liked "serious music." Meaning he was not listening to Johnny Mercer, or Louis Prima, or calypso with rum-and-Cokes, in 1946. They would have listened to Benjamin Britten. *Peter Grimes* opened in New York the week they got engaged. My father had taken a different girl, beautiful, wealthy, to see the Vienna Philharmonic at Carnegie Hall. He purposely bought the cheapest, highest seats, testing her seriousness about the music. She complained that they weren't in the loge; wasn't he serious about her? Instead he proposed to my mother.

The composer inks a whole note. Pauses. Flexes his wrist. I have a few minutes left to write. The cellos swim briskly; the room fills with the deep health of cellos. My coffee tastes like Prague, from a fire in a castle—

My mother said living with my father was like living alone. She liked to dance, liked flights of fancy. He seldom spoke. She might have loved someone who played "popular music." Flirted at night with her big band man, alone with Beethoven in the morning, on the hi-fi.

There is no crescendo, no end of the poem. My mother is dead. My father is with a woman who likes flamenco. The girl who makes coffee rinses out the sink: sound of water, hollow metal. The composer packs up his music. At the door, he is still moving his arm, conducting.

QUORUM

On the evening that their country was to go to war, the people gathered to decide what to do. Some wanted a nightly song. A forty-two-year-old woman squeezed a First Communion dress over her head and blessed a moth. There was no color associated with "fighting on my behalf." There were some wigs and hats left from the last quorum. The goats chewed them. Waitresses wanted to alter their recitation of the specials: Stuffed sea bass *a Menace at the Sky*; minestrone *and then a livid Claw*; dessert, *the Brahmic Vision*. A short journey into a place with trees, someone said. The old people and the small dogs shook, they thought shaking was enough. The cooks put away their silver bowls. The poets stopped cutting their hair. The firefighters asked why this night was different from all other nights. At eight o'clock their leader finished supper and declared war. What he ate was not documented.

SLIGHT PAUSE

We looked at each other, then at the plate of tomatoes,
and you said, do we eat them?

Our neighbor was dead. Fallen over in her front hall.
She had brought us green tomatoes.
Now they had ripened, they were heirlooms, they were heads
cut off and served to us
on a plate while we were going about our morning.

On the night of the earthquake, we ran to the Weather Channel
and then you said: are earthquakes weather?

Slight pause in which the world comes down.

We ate lavishly with salt and bread
our neighbor's still-warm tomatoes.

The night of the hanging, you said when does he hang?
as if you had asked, when is supper? We laughed
then checked online. The despot was hung in haste
for too few of his crimes
an hour ago while we were drinking wine.

EXCUSE ME, WHERE IS VARICK STREET?

Varick, yes. Just—oh Film Forum, sure.
Go straight down Carmine and turn left.
Wait, did I say to turn onto Houston after Varick?
Actually I'm walking that way.
You're welcome.
Actually you can turn here, before Varick:
this street dead-ends at Film Forum.
In fact, I'm going to Film Forum.
Would you like me to carry you?
I was going to carry something anyway.
Did I say to walk through the air molecules on the southwest corner of—?
Let's count forty blocks of sidewalk.
No, wait, thirty-seven paving stones to the corner.
The ticket window is there, on the south side of Houston.
Coincidentally, I'm also going to see the Tarkovsky.
I am ploughing and harrowing my soul,
rendering it capable of turning to good.
Two, please.
I was going to buy two tickets anyway, my pleasure.
The brownies here are delicious.
In fact I'm going to get one.
Here, let me feed it to you.
I am good for you.
I am good also for lost Japanese women,
For the boys in Big Brothers Big Sisters
(I am always seated next to them at weddings),
for the aggrieved,
the grieving, the recently blind—

Are you going to sit there?
Coincidentally I am also going to sit there.
Can you see out of my eyeholes? Are you comfortable?

A ROUND ORANGE JAM POT, AGAIN

A porcelain jam pot, dimpled all over, painted orange, with a porcelain stem. No one will mistake this for an orange. Count on china for cheer, not verisimilitude. Italians save the true-to-life for fresco swaddling, holy frescoed infants.

In our hotel dining room, a nicked, 12th-century table that resembles the distressed "Tuscan" furniture in mail order catalogues.

Travel is fun and this is how it looks: tourists solemnly buttering rolls and reading about the Duomo (too ornate and huge to evoke a personal religious fervor) or eating ham and talking about Pitti Palace, whose walls look like marble and are more valuable than marble in a country where marble is plentiful and people come to study the art of carving it. An almost perfect imitation of the real thing,

the cardboard buildings painted to look like stone for Hitler's visit to Rome. He was wowed. We are neither hardened nor saddened

by the morning television news; the war is new, the museums free of crowds.

Women in Chinese factories use hammers and dyes to make new tables look old. They are told to invent stories about the furniture so their nicks and stains make sense, i.e., a long time ago lived squid fishermen = faint blue wash, low spot from "fifty years of inky nets. . . ."

When I was twelve I wore a faithfully "rotted" apple-core necklace on a raw leather cord. It was wood, made to look gnawed. My friend Alda Giallombardo (neat in her Catholic school skirt) chose the alternate version: a pure white apple core, smooth as a doll crotch, on a delicate chain. More practical, she said.

47

Italian medieval armor was lustrous and shaped with elegance, but tragically flimsy. "In war the Italians themselves preferred German armor, which was ugly but practical. It was safer."

Unemployed German men can earn cash by flying to China and posing at factory openings. White men in suits, say the Chinese, make their products appealing to Chinese, who buy more shares. That, in turn, makes the company appealing to Germans, who buy more shares.

At home no one will ask whether we fought on our Italian tour. Weren't we silly with love, honeymooners owning the very airplane air? We will show them our new gloves.

I look beautiful when I cry, the woman at Piazza Gheberti says. I look beautiful crying, in Italian.

The walls of our hotel, in morning sun, are that yellow I have read about all my life. "Tuscan Yellow": I recognize it like the face of a friend! A paint color that almost captures this very minute: sun on yellow wall in spring, in Florence.

A LYNCHED MAN CAME WITH THE MAIL
ONTO MY DESK

A lynched man came with the mail onto my desk
In a crisp arts weekly

A bunch of grapes hangs above a kitchen counter in
An ad

For the gallery where the lynched man
Is hung   in this city

His eyes gaze upward   as if at a kite
His expression in death

Is polite
As if he might say something to your mother

That would make her nearly murmur
(Hands neat behind his back)

About the hard work of murder
The tree he hangs from leans

Into the frame   like a pet
What sort of poet

Would say that
A lynched man has the sturdiness of a left rake

49

JUST A SECOND AGO

I had an urge to toss my drink across the visiting poet's shirt.
   Hello. I liked your reading.
Red wine spreading into the whiteness
   It was a wonderful reading
of his shirt. My hand—my glass—
is still full.
     Yes. People starting to drift to the cheese and bread.
At the wedding, the organist stops,
the minister smiles benignantly. She thinks of touching the bride's breast.
   Hello. I liked your wedding.
It's amazing: traffic stays on its side of the road.
What keeps it there, really? I trust
no one will stand up and scream when I am a bride.
I don't laugh when I hear someone has died.
You're sitting there quietly right now

very
very quiet.

The slightest noise could cause an avalanche.

It's scary when someone gets pushed onto
   Hello. I liked your reading.
the subway tracks.
So scary when someone walks into Wendy's
and shoots the people eating.
     What I almost did
just a second ago
while you were crossing the street
while you were finishing your lunch
while you were handing me your terrible secret—

NANOPOEM

Little has arrived, with its pretty hatbox, to sit for you.

You can put it in your poem, send valentines to everything in the world:
little aunt's house, little rash, little Baltic shore, little raw thumb, little
humanitarian disaster.

You delivered yourself to little's fine, unencumbered, controllable void.
Look, there you are, size of an eyelash, slacks creased, and with a well-
shaped head, as after a C-section.

But turn on the lights in the tiny neon lounge:

Someone has stuffed cannons in there. Someone trashed the place,
peed on the bed. There's a herd of lambs afflicted with darling. They're
limping. Nothing but charmless lungs down in nanos, I've been there.
I turned the Holocaust into a pet. It slept in my lap, under a napkin.

If only there were room to birth a fullsize stallion and then, afterward,
assume your normal size. Gallop into troubled fields.

RESCUE SONG

What Do People Do All Day, Richard Scarry

FIRE! I read in my modern jazz radio
deejay voice. A cat mother screams,

her iron set the house aflame,
her cat-son plays, upstairs, alone—

My son has lived to be 4 and each morning asks for this story.
Keep reading, Mama. SAVE MY BOY!

I make the uppercase of emergency
gentle as the scent of laundry detergent.

A ladder claws the boy-cat's sill, I purr.
Purr the burning playroom door, the ax that chops it down.

Disaster solved. Wake/kiss/stir eggs: good morning love
at 9 a.m.

       Tell me again!
               I was in yoga when

people held hands and fell out of burning buildings downtown.
Commuters caught them on the small screens of their phones

tucked them into breast pockets and walked home.
Om.

What's happening, Mama? A nuclear accident (don't react)
being narrated on the radio, in Japanese.

A woman's voice like one of those paper flowers that blooms in water.
TRAPPED! the hashy simultaneous translation drowns her

elegant hush hush hush fatality onrush.
Morning brings fire, fire brings hoses full of cream.

When the EMTs do come—I wake up and can't move
wake up can't see wake up dead

he will kiss my knee and go to school. All's well.
Location of precinct. Location of alarm bell. Location of hydrant.

Location: our street in Brooklyn where, having dropped him
(as a baby) under a cab, I pray the driver will run over me too.

He will, he is a father, he understands—
Keep breathing.

The ambulance dazzles like a cocktail ring.
My boy leaps into the net on page 23.

SPOON REST OF THE EGYPTIANS

You never see a woman on the street and think hey, there's an Egyptian. Yesterday I saw an Inuit woman who looked like an Eskimo in a museum diorama, her soap-slab face even framed by a fur hood.

My friend R appears in certain paintings of the Italian Renaissance. See Tintoretto's *Portrait of a Woman Revealing Her Breasts*.

That man on the F train with the lunch pail, bloke cap, and sad black eyes, clearly boarded in 1940. But

this candy wrapper has not floated to us over the banks of the Nile.

Our parents never said what we feared: The temples are empty and always have been.

Kenneth Koch said: Imagine an Egyptian youth and that he speaks to you.

Here come the Egyptian children. They are offering us papyrus bookmarks in their flattened hands.

The Egyptologist says, this is the spoon rest. This the ignition switch, the birdhouse, the deck chair, the hair clip of the ancient Egyptians.

Nobody ever says: I know a great Egyptian restaurant . . .

In the Egypt Wing, schoolchildren run to sarcophagi, document the omens of the tombs, fall in love with the story of beer. Among the mummies, our children come to believe we won't forget them.

Our parents said to us, your forefathers were slaves in the land of Egypt.

Suffering—the history of splendor is false, but the history of suffering is real. If our parents had invented slave ancestors, they would have picked glamorous names for them, like Isis.

So, children, turn from the stories of queens, look at this carton of rings. Look at these piles of hair. The sneakers in this box look almost like the ones we wear.

MOTHER'S LOVE

1

Give the child up, says the warm blanket

Give the child up, says death, says
ruination, says torture, give the child up we will care for him
say the men with carapace faces

You can grieve, says the net
you are my favorite, says falling out a window

Grief has rules, says the raven, grief has grades,
sidelines, crowds to cheer you on
say the friendly faces smeared with dung

you can ace it, say the men with beetle-shell faces

2

The baby is tearing up tissues one by
one   each
in pieces with a strengthless
ripping

On my eyelids the fibers linger

Pale filaments of fairy dust, the hairs
of donkey ears
creatures under spells

The fairy makes a sound like cellophane

The baby answers in lighter-clicks
pah of little flame

The baby looks upward into a weather system
it settles round his head, a crown

He makes a sound like eyeliner coming wet and thin onto a brush
He makes a sound that wet and silken
you are getting very
young   you are getting very
                                        very

Wake mother wake this is how they take your baby
when you are drowsy with enticement—

3

His voice comes like a veil onto my eyes

Lightly a mother's bridal veil crumbles

The sweetness has come up to my collarbones
shows yellow under my chin
The mother is marked, tired. Tired and marked.

"Let's play on the bed"
(Don't speak, it will pull out the slow drip
anesthetic of his voice)

He pulls a book off the nightstand
I am helpless
We are addicts, an old boyfriend would say
This is not that. But it is
I am helpless

My hair fills with sparks

He is eating the rare book
curls the corner back so prettily

So what, say the hairs on my arms
so what, says the water rising in the room
He is melting all the books, tasting them
eating the corners—

In between, that sweet voice of no-words-yet

His sounds turn words to eyelashes, a fine fine net
a white powder

4

The baby pulls tissues from the box

Out!   and then
the next
one he pulls

that one   one more
with equal attention to them

all the pleasure is up to my skull
again the feel of my hair, new-cut, on my back
a rabbit asleep there

He pulls   pulls
a white, still rabbit from the box   he would
hold it up till it became vapor

The air gathers in pleats of vapor

I lie back

We are pulled together toward—
Are we alive on a planet

"My son and me"
(try to speak)

The words heavy as cured meat   can't push them
outward into the street the sun

The baby holds up an erasure
tears it, tears off a   room

5

floats over the edge of a breath
of a stand of milkweed

His breath exists as sand, slipping over my elbows

Water is pouring over the bed
Where is any fierceness

The traffic holds the house like a five-point harness

click

There is no traffic
no door   just the edge of an infinite pour

there is not even that

open your eyes

Anne says: "it is like mother's love"
(heroin)

What is it
I asked her
what does it feel like?

6

Alone with the baby is boring

woodfloors knees clockfalls
make rounds of hours

      Then the light, milkily, comes

We are sugared in a medium, he and I

He is smiling
Happiness is on me like a scratch in a car door

The floor is dirt and chalk
and cool as a henhouse

He has crawled into in the bathroom

                        "Can you open the door?"

                        "Can you close the door?"

The tub's cool slope
frames his head with stone

I smell like done bread

7

Turn over the loaf, tap tap—
hollow sound—door open.   He is smiling

A fishing line, clear, thin
drawn through my legs then tight across my chest
a line fine as a rapidograph
constant, narrow, even, drawn
round my wrists, shoulders, I am bound

back to front, tied up lightly in

8

in what
The light

is beautiful again.
Outside in the stopped air the animals have stopped.

The baby points at the light.
"?" he says
Answers sparkle and turn like coins on a line
Look at this look

how you are a fish-mother, silvery and still
on the pond-bottom
can't breach the surface where the boy
churns up hard light—

There is a spreading through me like snowmelt

9

He is in the milky world of the bathroom, the daytime
dry chill of it, he is suspended in marble

All at once he points at me

Then he is out the door, stepping onto a silver wing

How to describe to you this height, this opening?

HIS SOUNDS

13 months

Different-sized fiddleheads are questions coming up
and thinner-stemmed dandelions also
mean asking

Small scoops dig all the time into salt mounds

Being fine threads
and strings to tie up the meat
and lengths of rat-tail cord
his sounds bind me to him

Wrinkling tissue is a fraction
of the pleasure he takes in chrome

Alert!

Unhappy/somewhat
in the form of wet static
a radio in a storm

[In the front seat I say to myself
is somebody
back there?
Because how can it be there
is somebody back there? . . .]

A spine made of moths, wings pulsing

Dried leaves scrape over my neck

Next comes a long unfolding of a map

An antique piece of machine
goes around
and around
lever cold in the hand
slow, slow
            slower

A stream of rusted water:
that's him coming to a stop

Better hurry home

ALL YOU DO IS PERCEIVE

I was given a city, with coffee and sunlight. "The coin-purse smell of the subway," I wrote. In the mornings policemen would stand, lightstruck and pleasured, over trays of danish. Mornings I wrote and workmen raised up their nets. Hallelujah the brick, the debris! I was given a city. The city got between me and God.

I was given a house. The curtains breathed over wide sills. There was a leaf in the middle of the floor, I loved the crispness of the leaf. I loved the privacy of sills. The sills sailed, I fell into the sills. The sills got between me and God.

I was given a mud hut. The walls curved to meet the ceiling like a tongue curves to make a word.

I was given God, with salt and sweet together. I was given a piece of meat. I loved the flesh. I was given bread only. I was given only water. I loved the coolness of the water. The water got between me and the feast.

I had an empty plate and there was the color of it. I cannot even describe the color of it.

I was given a cell with a window. There was a certain light at evening.

I was given nothing but the air, and the air dazzled.

NOTES

"Which from That Time Infus'd Sweetness into my Heart": the title, and "What seemed fair in all the world," come from John Milton's *Paradise Lost*; "Till at last, pop!" from Kenneth Grahame's *Wind in the Willows*; "While thou on press'd flowers dost sleep," *A Midsummer Night's Dream* (3.1.153). "Death Is Something Entirely Else": "Struck from thin glasses successively at random" is from Marianne Moore's poem "Those Various Scalpels." "My Life": the dress, as worn by journalist Nellie Bly on her 1889 race around the globe; John Wesley Powell (dir. U.S. Geological Survey) noted that he saw "three Mormons and an Indian" fishing as he came out of the Colorado River canyon at the end of his expedition of 1869 (Powell, the first human to pass through the canyon, had been presumed dead). "Suicide Cascade," for Sarah Hannah. "Study of a Friend With One Breast," for Prudence. "December, Fever": special thanks to Dan Lakamp. "Big Baby": Mr. Crispsparkle, "early riser, musical, classical," a lover of swimming, is a character in Charles Dickens' unfinished novel *The Mystery of Edwin Drood*. "The Imagination, Drunk with Prohibitions": the title is from W. C. Williams' *Spring and All*. "[Noon, F Train]": The quoted line is from C.D. Wright's poem "Like Peaches." "Quorum": The italicized phrases are Emily Dickinson's. "Slight Pause": the execution of Saddam Hussein, Dec. 30, 2006. "Excuse Me, Where Is Varick Street?": "I am ploughing and harrowing my soul, rendering it capable of turning to good" quotes Andrei Tarkovsky's idea about the purpose of art. "A Round Orange Jam Pot, Again": the quote is from Luigi Barzini's *The Italians*. "Rescue Song" refers to page 23 of Richard Scarry's children's book *What Do People Do All Day?* "All You Do Is Perceive": "Perceive! That's all you do. Perceive," as delivered by David Pittu in the 2005 Atlantic Theatre Company revival of Harold Pinter's *The Room*.

I am indebted to my son for teaching me new habits of regarding; to the friends and fellow writers whose generous perceptions helped shape these poems; and to the National Endowment for the Arts, who gave me funds, which became time and materials, to write and edit some of this work.

ACKNOWLEDGMENTS

I wish to thank the editors and supporters of these journals, in which some of these poems, or versions of them, first appeared:

American Poetry Review, Bengal Lights, Blackbird, Black Clock, Bomb, Boulevard, Cincinnati Review, Colorado Review, Conduit, Court Green, Eleven Eleven, 42opus, Gulf Coast, Margie, Ms., Nextbook.org, Notre Dame Review, Ploughshares, Quarterly West, and *Verse.*

"December, Fever" was reprinted in in *Pushcart Prize XXXVI: Best of the Small Presses.* "My Life" was reprinted in *Verse: the Second Decade.* "Just a Second Ago" appeared in *The Best American Poetry* 2006; "Death Is Something Entirely Else" in *The Best American Poetry* 2012 (series ed. David Lehman, guest eds. Billy Collins and Mark Doty, respectively). "His Sounds" was printed in 2012 as a broadside by All Along Press in conjunction with the Fort Gondo Poetry Series in St. Louis. "All You Do Is Perceive" was reprinted in the 2013 Argos Poetry Calendar, published by Argos Books. "Which from That Time Infus'd Sweetness into My Heart" was reprinted as a chapbook by Argos Books. My gratitude to these editors, curators, and artists.

Joy Katz is the author of two previous poetry collections. A former Wallace Stegner and National Endowment for the Arts fellow, she lives in Pittsburgh, Pa., where she teaches in the graduate writing program at Chatham University. More information can be found at www.joykatz.com.